ADVANCED VIOLIN SCALE STUDIES

I0801787

ELAINE FINE

MEL BAY

WWW.MELBAY.COM

Introduction

Practicing scales is vital for building and maintaining technique. Through scale practice, we learn to navigate the fingerboard, shift from position to position, develop bow control, improve intonation, develop strength, and develop a vibrant and varied sound.

We all approach the practice of scales with the best of intentions, but at some point in the process, particularly when they begin and end on the tonic note and ascend and descend with proscribed fingerings and bowing patterns, we can shut off our ears and minds and play automatically. While it is possible to develop strength, agility, and muscle memory through automatic scale playing, it is very easy to play them without being intellectually or musically engaged; we may not really pay attention to the way different keys feel and sound on the violin, or even to what particular scale we happen to be playing.

The pieces in this book are musically, intellectually, and rhythmically challenging one-page lyrical compositions that move stepwise through each of the major and minor keys. The first twenty-four follow the circle of fifths, with the minor scale preceding its relative major. Everything moves stepwise, with pitches repeated at pitch level and at the octave. The stepwise motion and octave jumps make navigation from one pitch to the next easy to hear, even when playing in keys with many sharps or flats.

Each piece is named for an animal that has scales. The three squirrels have the same musical material in different keys. The pieces named for members of the snake, crocodile, butterfly, fish, bird, lizard, and pangolin families share material, but they employ a lot of variation. The butterfly pieces all use a *tresillo* rhythm that divides the meter of 8/8 into asymmetrical groups of threes and twos.

There are occasional string indications of where a passage should be played, but I have left the fingering choices to the violinist (or the teacher). There are no metronome markings indicated, only Italian (and sometimes English) suggestions of character. These pieces can be practiced at comfortable tempos with a metronome, but as solo concert pieces they should be played with expressive freedom.

I hope that practicing these pieces and learning about these animals will spark the creative imaginations of the people who play them, and as people become more engaged with the expressive musical qualities that scales have to offer, they might be inspired to write scale pieces of their own.

Elaine Fine

Contents

Cloudless Sulphur Butterfly

Phoebis sennae

A minor

Allegro semplice

Elaine Fine

Cameroon Scaly-Tail Squirrel

Zenkerella insignis

C major

Red-Tailed Boa

Boa constrictor

E minor

Green Iguana

Iguana iguana

G major

Allegretto

Saw-Scaled Viper

Anilius scytale

B minor

Sprezzatura

Red Factor Canary

Serinius carnria domestica

D major

Sprightly

(LH pizz. on lower pitch only.)

Funereal Duskywing Butterfly

Erynnis funeralis

F-sharp minor

American Crocodile

Crocodylus acutus

A major

Gorgon Copper Butterfly

Lycaena gorgono

C-sharp minor

Steller's Sea Eagle

Haliaeetus pelagicus

E major

Lembert's Green Hairstreak

Callophrys sherindanii lemberti

G-sharp minor

Lord Darby's Scaly-Tailed Squirrel

Anomalurus derebianus

B major

Giant Pangolin

Smutsia gigantea

D-sharp minor

Barcarolle

Freshwater Crocodile

Crocodylus jonsoni

F-sharp major

Brightly

This can also be played half a step lower in F major by replacing the sharps in the key signature with a single B flat.

Blowfish

Diodon antennatus

B-flat minor

Cuban Crocodile

Crocodylus rhombifer

C-sharp major

Try it in C major as well. Just remove all the sharps.

Rainbow Sardine

Dussumieria acuta

F minor

Brightly flickering
a piacere

Musky Rat-Kangaroo

Hypsiprymnodon moschatus

A-flat major

This can also be played in A major by replacing the four flats in the key signature with three sharps.

Great White Shark

Carcharoden Carcharias

C minor

Agitato

Blue Scaled Quail

Callipepla squamata

E-flat major

Brahminy Blind Snake

Indotyphlops braminus

G minor

Tokay Gecko

Gekko gecko

B-flat major

Neon Damselfish

Pomacentrus coelestis

D minor

Quasi sarabande

Pel's Flying Squirrel

Anomalurus pelii

F major

False Coral Snake

Anilius scytale

A minor

Sanford's Sea Eagle

Haliaeetus sanfordi

E-flat major

Black-Bellied Pangolin

Phataginus tetradactyla

D minor

Round Sardinella

Sardinella aurita

F major

Northern Bobwhite

Colinus virginianus

E major